X 1/13   1112 LAST   CR

D0819832

BLUE BANNER
BIOGRAPHY

LUDACRIS

Joanne Mattern

Mitchell Lane

PUBLISHERS

P.O. Box 196
Hockessin, Delaware 19707
Visit us on the web: www.mitchelllane.com
Comments? email us: mitchelllane@mitchelllane.com

Printing   1   2   3   4   5   6   7   8   9

Blue Banner Biographies

Alicia Keys	Gwen Stefani	Megan Fox
Allen Iverson	Ice Cube	Miguel Tejada
Ashanti	Ja Rule	Nancy Pelosi
Ashlee Simpson	Jamie Foxx	Natasha Bedingfield
Ashton Kutcher	Jay-Z	Orianthi
Avril Lavigne	Jennifer Lopez	Orlando Bloom
Beyoncé	Jessica Simpson	P. Diddy
Blake Lively	J. K. Rowling	Peyton Manning
Bow Wow	Joe Flacco	Pink
Brett Favre	John Legend	Prince William
Britney Spears	Justin Berfield	Queen Latifah
CC Sabathia	Justin Timberlake	Rihanna
Carrie Underwood	Kanye West	Robert Downey Jr.
Chris Brown	Kate Hudson	Robert Pattinson
Chris Daughtry	Katy Perry	Ron Howard
Christina Aguilera	Keith Urban	Sean Kingston
Ciara	Kelly Clarkson	Selena
Clay Aiken	Kenny Chesney	Shakira
Cole Hamels	Ke$ha	Shia LaBeouf
Condoleezza Rice	Kristen Stewart	Shontelle Layne
Corbin Bleu	Lady Gaga	Soulja Boy Tell 'Em
Daniel Radcliffe	Lance Armstrong	Stephenie Meyer
David Ortiz	Leona Lewis	Taylor Swift
David Wright	Lil Wayne	T.I.
Derek Jeter	Lindsay Lohan	Timbaland
Drew Brees	Ludacris	Tim McGraw
Eminem	Mariah Carey	Toby Keith
Eve	Mario	Usher
Fergie	Mary J. Blige	Vanessa Anne Hudgens
Flo Rida	Mary-Kate and Ashley Olsen	Zac Efron

Library of Congress Cataloging-in-Publication Data
Mattern, Joanne, 1963–
  Ludacris / by Joanne Mattern.
    p. cm. — (Blue banner biographies)
  Includes bibliographical references and index.
  ISBN 978-1-61228-055-4 (library bound)
  1. Ludacris (Rapper—Juvenile literature. 2. Rap musicians—United States—Biography—Juvenile literature. I. Title.
  ML3930.L85M37 2012
  782.42164902—dc22
  [B]
                                                                                    2011016776
eBook ISBN: 9781612281827

PARENTS AND TEACHERS STRONGLY CAUTIONED:
The story of Ludacris' life may not be appropriate for youger readers.

ABOUT THE AUTHOR: Joanne Mattern is the author of more than 250 books for children. She has written biographies about many famous people for Mitchell Lane, including *Ashley Tisdale*, *Peyton Manning*, *The Jonas Brothers*, *LeBron James*, and *Drake Bell and Josh Peck*. Joanne also enjoys writing about animals, reading, and being outdoors. She lives in New York State with her husband, four children, and several pets.

PUBLISHER'S NOTE: The following story has been thoroughly researched, and to the best of our knowledge represents a true story. While every possible effort has been made to ensure accuracy, the publisher will not assume liability for damages caused by inaccuracies in the data and makes no warranty on the accuracy of the information contained herein. This story has not been authorized or endorsed by Chris Bridges, aka Ludacris.

Blue Banner Biography

Ludacris faced poverty as a child, but he took advantage of opportunities to hone his skills and talents in the music and

Looking for Trouble

*F*ans and entertainers who gathered on November 16, 2005, for the VIBE Awards expected to hear great music and see some of the biggest stars of hip-hop, rap, and soul music. The awards, sponsored by *VIBE* magazine, were always exciting. Sometimes the awards featured controversy as well. This was one of those times.

When rap star Ludacris came out to perform the song "Georgia," he wore a leather jacket and a hoodie. Both featured images of the Confederate flag. This flag is the symbol of the Confederate nation, which was made up of Southern states who seceded, or left, the Union during the early 1860s. This action led to the Civil War between 1861 and 1865. Because the South was proslavery, the Confederate flag has become a symbol of racism and violence against African Americans. Viewers were shocked when Ludacris, an African American, came out with the flag on his clothes.

When Ludacris finished his performance, he took off the Confederate flag and stomped on it. Once again, fans were not sure what to think. What was the young artist trying to say?

Ludacris' tough-guy image is not an act, but he adds a sense of humor and fun to his gritty lyrics.

Ludacris certainly understood what the Confederate flag stands for. He chose to wear it that night for a very special reason. After the show, he explained his actions in a statement to the media. "This flag represents the oppression that we as African Americans have endured for years; this is a symbol of segregation and the racism that reigned not only throughout the South but throughout the United States. I wore it to represent where we came from, to remind people that Ray Charles's original 'Georgia' was written because of that racism."

Ludacris went on to discuss the bigger picture. "Racism is just as prevalent now, and if we are not constantly mindful of our history and take charge of it, history is destined to repeat itself because of ignorance. In order to move forward, we must never forget where we were." Ludacris wanted everyone to know that the racism that had existed during the Civil War is still alive. He wore the flag to raise awareness about how African Americans are still treated unfairly and how unacceptable that kind of behavior is.

Ludacris has never been afraid to say or do what he believes is right. He does not worry about what people think of him.

Artistically, Ludacris has never been afraid to say or do what he believes is right. He does not worry about what people think of him. He cares about being true to himself and doing his best for his fans. This attitude has helped make him one of rap's biggest stars and has brought him success as an actor as well.

CHAPTER 2

Growing Up Hip-Hop

*C*hristopher Brian Bridges was born on September 11, 1977, in Champaign, Illinois. His parents, Roberta Shields and Wayne Brian Bridges, were college students when Chris was born.

Hip-hop was very popular when Chris was young, and he quickly became a fan of this type of music. Hip-hop music was born in the 1970s in the Bronx, which is part of New York City. Originally called rap, this new style of music featured a DJ (disc jockey) spinning records and repeating the parts of songs that included the rhythm section, or beat. At the same time, a performer called an MC (master of ceremonies) created a type of poetry called rap, which was spoken over the music. These raps usually included clever wordplay or rhymes and often focused on everyday subjects such as life in the neighborhood, trouble with the police, or falling in love. Rappers often performed at gatherings called house jams.

Some of Chris's earliest memories included music. His parents often went to house jams, and they usually brought little Chris with them. Ludacris later recalled, "My parents were always jamming to the old school stuff. They used to take me to college parties and let me get out in the middle of the floor and dance for all the other students. My parents always knew, from way back, that I'd be an entertainer. I used to perform in the living room when I was barely walking, so they knew this was coming."

Chris quickly became a fan of rap music, and soon he was creating his own songs. In 2002, he told a reporter from *Teen People* magazine, "I wrote my first rap song when I was nine years old. I said, 'I'm cool, I'm bad, I might be 10, but I can't survive without my girlfriend.' And I was only nine, but I needed something to rhyme with 'girlfriend.' I didn't even have one!"

Chris's parents split up when he was young, but both of them have remained a big part of his life. Chris remembers that his father often bought him records and introduced him to new hip-hop artists. When he was twelve years old, Chris joined his first hip-hop group. The group, called Loudmouth Hooligans, was based in the nearby city of Chicago.

"My mom was very strict. She disciplined me . . . ." She also made sure he stayed in school and studied hard.

However, Chris's time with the Loudmouth Hooligans did not last long. Soon after he joined, Chris and his mother moved to Atlanta, Georgia.

Times were difficult in Atlanta. In an interview with the *San Francisco Chronicle*, Chris recalled living with his mom in one room in somebody else's house. He and his mother often lived in poor, rough neighborhoods, and Chris saw many young men fall into a life of drugs and crime. However, his mother would not let Chris follow that path. "My mom was very strict," he told the *Chronicle* reporter. "She disciplined me, taught me a lot about bank accounts, about saving money." She also made sure he stayed in school and studied hard.

Even though Roberta Shields was strict and made sure Chris stayed out of trouble, she let him have fun. His favorite way to kick around was to perform. Soon after he moved to Atlanta, he began rapping in school and around the neighborhood. He also began performing in talent shows and

Ludacris' poor childhood made him want to give back to children in the same situation. In May 2010, Ludacris helped build a playground at Venetian Hills Elementary School in his hometown of Atlanta.

Roberta Shields (left) has always been a huge influence in her son's life. She supported his musical dreams but made sure Chris stayed away from drugs and got a good education.

at open mic nights at local clubs. These performances gave him valuable experience in performing in front of a crowd. That talent would serve him well in the years to come.

CHAPTER 3

Breaking Into the Business

Chris graduated from high school in 1995. He had a big decision to make. All he wanted to do was perform, and he was determined to break into the music business. He wasn't sure that going to college was the best way to achieve his dreams.

Chris's parents and other family members had a different idea. They encouraged him to go to college. Chris knew that education was important, so he enrolled at Georgia State University. Four years later, he graduated with a degree in music management.

Chris did more than study the business, though. While he was in college, he worked as an intern at an Atlanta radio station called Hot 97.5. During an internship, a person works for free in exchange for college credit. It didn't take long for the people at Hot 97.5 to realize Chris was talented. Soon he was rapping on commercials for the station. Listeners loved his raps, and Chris gained many fans. After a short time, he was offered a job on the air as a DJ.

Like many DJs at the station, Chris came up with a nickname: Chris Luva Luva. He had a great time being on the air. One of his favorite things to do was make up his own lyrics to the songs he played. His fans loved his show and Chris became well known in the Atlanta rap scene. Working as a DJ also gave him the chance to meet well-known musicians and producers. One of his most exciting moments was meeting famous hip-hop producer Timbaland. Timbaland liked the young rapper's talent. In 1998, he produced an album that featured Chris's rapping on a song called "Phat Rabbit."

Chris Luva Luva was on the air for three years. During that time, he learned all he could about the music business. He learned how to run sound equipment and the responsibilities of producers and recording engineers. He also learned how record companies choose new artists and how they market their music to the public. As he worked, Chris saved his money so that he could produce his own rap album. Finally, in 2000, he was ready. He just needed one more thing to start his rap career: a new name.

> *Working as a DJ also gave him the chance to meet well-known musicians and producers.*

Chris decided to call himself Ludacris, which plays off his name, Chris, and the word *ludicrous*. As he explained to a writer for *Ebony* magazine, "*Ludacris* means crazy and wild and ridiculous. My music is a little fun in people's lives." He told another interviewer on the radio program *Showcase*, "I have kind of a split personality—part of me is calm, cool, and collected, while the other side is just beyond crazy. My lyrics

Ludacris loves his hometown of Atlanta and often appears at events in the city. On May 14, 2011, he performed at a Civil Rights Day event at an Atlanta Braves baseball game. He introduced civil rights legend Jesse Jackson during the song "Welcome to Atlanta."

are ludicrous, my live shows are ludicrous—ludicrous like off-the-chain crazy."

In 2000, Ludacris released his first album, *Incognegro*, on his own label, which he called Disturbing Tha Peace. Even though it is almost impossible to succeed with an album that is not on a major record label, Chris had a plan. He used his popularity as Chris Luva Luva to build interest in the album, and he drove to rap shows and sold copies of it out of the trunk of his car. Thanks to his hard work, *Incognegro* beat the odds. Within a year, it had sold 50,000 copies and was a huge hit in Atlanta.

Major record labels soon heard about Ludacris and his unlikely success. At that time, Atlanta was the center of a hip-hop movement called Dirty South. Def Jam, the most popular hip-hop record label, wanted to get in on Dirty South's popularity. The label signed Ludacris to a recording contract.

In 2001, Def Jam released *Back for the First Time*, a re-release of *Incognegro* with some new songs added. The album became a huge hit, selling more than three million copies nationwide and reaching number four on the Billboard Top 200 Chart. The album featured the hit singles "What's Your Fantasy" and "Southern Hospitality." Ludacris was able to work with Timbaland again on this album, as well as other well-known rappers, including Foxy Brown and UGK. *Back for the First Time* was nominated for a Grammy for Best Rap Album.

Ludacris quickly went back into the studio. His next album, *Word of Mouf*, came out just a few months after *Back for the First Time*. *Word of Mouf* also sold more than three million copies. Ludacris was here to stay.

> **Def Jam, the most popular hip-hop record label, wanted to get in on Dirty South's popularity.**

CHAPTER 4

Controversy and Success

*L*udacris had become famous well beyond Atlanta. Fans all over the nation loved his music, but not everyone was a fan of his sound or his lyrics.

Many of the words to Ludacris's songs are not pretty. He raps about violence and sex. He often uses profanity. His lyrics are not unusual for the Dirty South style of hip-hop, but many people do not like them.

In 2002, Pepsi hired Ludacris to be in its commercials. Television talk-show host Bill O'Reilly spoke out against the move. He said Pepsi was sending a bad message to America's youth because it was promoting music by a "gangsta rapper." He convinced people not to buy Pepsi's products. Pepsi quickly dropped the commercials and ended its association with Ludacris. The artist was angry and spoke out against the decision. He said in a statement that was released to the media, "I don't feel as if Pepsi values the black dollar because of what they did." Other people spoke out in support of Ludacris and hip-hop music. They said that hip-hop gave a voice to disadvantaged people and allowed them to share their experiences about racism, violence, and poverty.

Ludacris did not let his critics stop him. In 2003, he released his next album, *Chicken-n-Beer*, featuring the hit song "Stand Up." This song, about partying in a club, was produced by hip-hop superstar Kanye West and went to number one on the Billboard Hot 100 chart.

His 2004 album, *The Red Light District*, was a big step forward for Ludacris and showed how much he had grown as a rapper. He explained to *Rolling Stone* that year, "I think that with every album you have to give people a piece of you, something they don't know about; whether it's personal or maybe a sound or idea they haven't heard before. That's something I set out to do this time. . . . On this album, I talk about everything. I get personal about my emotions, money, situations, my life."

For example, in "Number One Spot," the second single from that album, he sends a message to Bill O'Reilly:

> I'm never goin' nowhere so don't
>   try me
> My music sticks in fans' veins like an IV
> Flows poison like Ivy, oh they grimy
> Already offers on my 6th album from labels tryin' to
>   sign me
> Respected highly, HIIII MR. O'REILLY
> Hope all is well, . . .

"I think that with every album you have to give people a piece of you, something they don't know about."

The Grammys have honored Ludacris several times for his rap songs and albums. "I always dreamed big because in order to be successful you have to dream big," he told Ebony *magazine.*

Fans loved *The Red Light District*, and so did many music critics. In 2004 and 2005, Ludacris was nominated for several awards for his work, including BET's Viewer Choice Award and an MTV Music Award for Best Rap Video for his song "Number One Spot."

Ludacris was thrilled to win a Grammy in 2005. He had been nominated several times over the years and finally won for Best Rap/Sung Collaboration for "Yeah," which he recorded with two other rap stars, Usher and Lil Jon.

Ludacris continued to tour and record. However, he was ready to expand his talents. Using his real name, Chris Bridges, Ludacris entered the movie business and turned out to have a lot of talent in that area, too.

In his first film appearance, which was in 2001, he had a small role in *The Wash*, a film that featured several hip-hop performers, including Dr. Dre and Snoop Dogg. In 2003, he had a major role in the action film *2 Fast 2 Furious*, about a former police officer who gets caught up in an undercover caper to bring down a drug lord. Bigger roles were about to arrive.

Ludacris shows off his wild side while filming the video for his song "Act a Fool" from the 2003 movie 2 Fast 2 Furious. *Ludacris also acted in the film under his real name, Chris Bridges.*

In 2004, Ludacris appeared as a carjacker in the movie *Crash*. The movie featured several Hollywood stars, including Don Cheadle, Sandra Bullock, Thandie Newton, and Matt Dillon. At first, Ludacris was worried about appearing with such experienced actors. He told the *San Francisco Chronicle*, "Once I heard about all the people who were going to be a part of it, I knew I had to step up to the plate, because I was the least experienced actor in it."

He also faced the challenge of playing a character who is very different from himself. The character, Anthony, is a carjacker who hates hip-hop culture and claims that the music was created by white people in order to stereotype African Americans and make them look bad.

Ludacris and his Crash *costars Matt Dillon, Don Cheadle, Terrence Howard, and Larenz Tate won Screen Actors Guild (SAG) Awards in 2006. Ludacris takes his acting and his music careers seriously and knows that talent is more important than image. He says, "Your ego can't get bigger than yourself and the things you're trying to do."* Hustle & Flow *with Terrence Howard was also nominated for the same award.*

Ludacris' movie roles aren't all serious. In 2007 he played DJ Donnie in the Christmas comedy Fred Claus.

Even though he was a famous hip-hop star, he was not afraid to ask the other actors for help. Terrence Howard, who also appeared in the film, told an interviewer from MTV that Ludacris "asked for advice on every part of this thing. . . . I have the utmost respect for Chris Bridges the actor."

Crash was a commercial and critical success, winning an Academy Award for Best Picture in 2006. Also that year, Chris and his cast mates won a Screen Actors Guild Award for Outstanding Performance by a Cast in a Motion Picture.

Just a few months after *Crash* was released, Ludacris and Howard appeared in another major film. *Hustle & Flow* is about the hip-hop music scene, and Ludacris had a small but important role as a successful rap artist. The film was a big success, and critics and fans alike praised Ludacris's performance. It was clear that his talents went well beyond the music scene.

Ludacris' charitable foundation has helped children and familie all over Atlanta. Ludacris is proud to use his influence to help people in need and encourage others to do the same.

Giving Back

*I*n 2006, Ludacris released his next album, *Release Therapy*. This one was more serious than his earlier work. For the first time, he commented on society in his music, and some of his lyrics were grim. However, the album still featured raw and intense raps and lighthearted party songs. The first single, "Money Maker" reached number one on the Billboard Hot 100 Chart. The album was another huge success and won the 2007 Grammy Award for Best Rap Album.

Although Ludacris still loved rapping, he became more interested in acting. He added television credits to his accomplishments when he appeared on the hit TV show *Law & Order: Special Victims Unit* in 2006 and 2007. "Music will always pump through my veins. But I see acting as something I want to do more in the future," he told a reporter from the *Boston Herald*. In 2007, he appeared in the comedy *Fred Claus*. In 2008, he appeared in the action film *RocknRolla*. Jumping ahead to 2011, he made a well-received appearance in the hit romantic comedy *No Strings Attached*, which stars Ashton Kutcher and Natalie Portman.

Meanwhile Ludacris continued to make music. He released *Theater of the Mind* in 2008. This album featured a number of rap celebrities, including Chris Brown, Lil Wayne, Rick Ross, Common, Jay-Z, and The Game.

Battle of the Sexes was released in 2010. The album highlighted different points of view between men and women. "Hip-hop is such a male-dominated industry," Ludacris told *USA Today* in 2010. "There's a female voice that's sometimes missing." To give women their say, Ludacris invited many female rappers to perform on the album, including Eve, Lil' Kim, Shawnna, and Nicki Minaj.

Ludacris' acting career continues to shine. In 2011 he appeared with two of Hollywood's hottest stars, Ashton Kutcher and Natalie Portman, in the romantic comedy No Strings Attached.

Battle of the Sexes became Ludacris' fourth number-one album on the Billboard Top 200 Chart, and it spent six weeks at number one on the Top Rap Albums Chart, selling more than 530,000 copies. The first single from the album, "How Low," was a huge hit. Meanwhile, he began work on his next album, *Ludaversal*.

The rapper admits he rarely stops working. "I'm always in that mode—whenever I have a little free time, I'm always recording songs, writing, whatever I gotta do. It's like my job is my vacation."

Ludacris also likes to help other musicians. His record label, Disturbing Tha Peace, or DTP, allows him to guide artists who are just starting their careers. Ludacris has never been afraid to try something new, so DTP represents more than rappers. In 2005, rhythm and blues artist Bobby Valentino released his album, *Bobby Valentino*, on Disturbing Tha Peace, and in 2007 its follow-up, *Special Occasion*, was released. Both albums were well-received and featured several hit singles. Ludacris told MTV, "With DTP, we never want to be limited to what we do." He also told VH1, "I'm always trying to position myself to where I'm broadening my horizons."

Broadening his horizons includes helping people who are not as fortunate as he. In 2001, Ludacris and his mother started the Ludacris Foundation. Within ten years, the foundation had given out more than $1.5 million to support Atlanta charities, food banks, and back-to-school programs.

> *". . . whenever I have a little free time, I'm always recording songs, writing, whatever I gotta do. It's like my job is my vacation."*

Ludacris' daughter, Karma, was born in 2001. "Having a little girl has forced me to broaden my horizons when it comes to women," he wrote on his web site. He also wanted to open the public's eyes to the talents of female rappers. "We want to hear women talk more about what women do as opposed to trying to be like men or talk about what men do," he said of female rappers.

Ludacris sometimes joins foundation volunteers by going out into communities and handing out boxes of food to families in need. "I'm blessed to have so much, and the more power and more influence I have, the more I want to give back and reach back," he told *USA Today* in 2010. "I love leading by example, and if other people see me doing this, hopefully they'll be inspired to help out."

Ludacris has also worked with the National Network for Youth and the National Runaway Switchboard. He urges teens to reach out to these resources if they face abuse or other troubles at home. "This is not just a runaway problem; this is my problem, this is your problem—this is our problem," he told *Jet* magazine in 2006. Ludacris credits the birth of his daughter, Karma, in 2001, with making him see that every child needs to learn self-respect and have a chance to succeed. Karma's mother, Christine White, is an Atlanta lawyer who has had an on-again, off-again relationship with Ludacris over the years.

Ludacris is also a member of HSAN, the Hip-Hop Summit Action Network. Through HSAN, he has joined with other rap stars, such as Mary J. Blige and Russell Simmons, to stress the importance of education and literacy.

By the beginning of 2011, Chris "Ludacris" Bridges had sold more than 15 million albums and appeared in award-winning movies. He had also helped thousands of people

> *"I'm blessed to have so much, and the more power and more influence I have, the more I want to give back and reach back."*

through his charity work. Throughout his efforts, he has always remained true to himself and his emotions. The artist has a simple explanation for his hard work and success: "It's just the rush that I get from working toward a goal and really loving what I do," he told *USA Today*. "I love it so much it's almost a crime, because not everybody is so blessed. I will keep going until I can't do any more."

1977	Christopher Brian Bridges is born on September 11 in Champaign, Illinois.
1989	Bridges joins his first hip-hop group, the Loudmouth Hooligans; soon afterward he moves to Atlanta.
1996	He begins working at radio station Hot 97.5 under the DJ name Chris Luva Luva.
2000	He produces his first album, *Incognegro*, and begins performing under the name Ludacris. He starts his record label, Disturbing Tha Peace (DTP). He is signed by Def Jam Records.
2001	Def Jam re-releases *Incognegro* under the title *Back for the First Time*, and the album goes triple platinum; it is nominated for a Grammy for Best Rap Album. He and his mother establish the Ludacris Foundation.
2003	He appears in the movie *2 Fast 2 Furious*.
2004	Ludacris is nominated for an MTV Music Video Award for Breakthrough Male Performance.
2005	He creates controversy when he wears the Confederate flag at the VIBE awards. He appears in the movies *Crash* and *Hustle & Flow*. He wins his first Grammy Award for Best Rap/Sung Collaboration ("Yeah," Usher featuring Lil Jon and Ludacris).
2006	Ludacris is nominated Best Actor by BET. He and his costars win a Screen Actors Guild Award for Outstanding Performance by a Cast in a Motion Picture for *Crash*; he makes his first appearance on the TV show *Law & Order: Special Victims Unit* in the episode "Venom."
2007	Ludacris wins a Grammy for Best Rap Album for *Release Therapy*.
2008	He releases the album *Theater of the Mind* and appears in the movie *RocknRolla*.
2010	Ludacris releases the album *Battle of the Sexes*.
2011	He releases the album *Ludaversal* and appears in the movies *Fast Five* and *No Strings Attached*.

FILMOGRAPHY

2011	*Fast Five*	**2005**	*The Heart of the Game*
	No Strings Attached		*Hustle & Flow*
2009	*Gamer*	**2004**	*Crash*
2008	*Ball Don't Lie*	**2003**	*2 Fast 2 Furious*
	RocknRolla		*Paper Chasers* (documentary)
	Max Payne		
2007	*Fred Claus*	**2001**	*The Wash*

DISCOGRAPHY

2011	*Ludaversal*	**2001**	*Back for the First Time*
2010	*Battle of the Sexes*		*Word of Mouf*
2008	*Theater of the Mind*	**2000**	*Incognegro*
2006	*Release Therapy*		
2004	*The Red Light District*		
2003	*Chicken-n-Beer*		

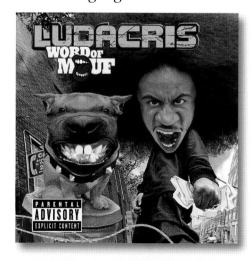

FURTHER READING

Books

Scott, Celicia. *Ludacris*. Broomall, Pennsylvania: Mason Crest Publishers, 2007.

Torres, John Albert. *Timbaland*. Hockessin, Delaware: Mitchell Lane Publishers, 2008.

Wolny, Philip. *Ludacris*. New York: Rosen Publishing Group, 2009.

Works Consulted

"5 Questions for: Ludacris." (Front Row) *Ebony*, August 1, 2003.

Caramanica, Jon. "Ludacris: It's Not All Jokes and Rhymes." *Teen People*, Summer 2002 Music Supplement, Vol. 5.

Carroll, Larry. "Chris 'Ludacris' Bridges: Movie Star." MTV Features and Interviews, n.d. http://www.mtv.com/shared/movies/features/c/crash_ludacris_050502/

Hart, Hugh. "Ludacris' Crash Course in Acting." *SFGate [San Francisco Chronicle, Internet Edition]*, May 8, 2005. http://articles.sfgate.com/2005-05-08/entertainment/17371356_1_chris-ludacris-bridges-don-cheadle-los-angeles

Hoffman, Melody K. "Ludacris: Hit-Maker Shares Personal Side with Community and Fans." *Jet*, December 11, 2006, Vol. 110, Issue 23.

Jones, Steve. "Multitasker Ludacris Runs His Own Show." *USA Today*, March 9, 2010. http://www.usatoday.com/life/music/news/2010-03-09-ludacris09_CV_N.htm

" 'Leading by Example' in Charity Work." *USA Today*, March 9, 2010. http://www.usatoday.com/LIFE/usaedition/2010-03-09-ludacris09_VA_U.htm

"Ludacris Says He Wanted Lauryn Hill for 'Sexes' CD." *Yahoo Music*, March 26, 2010. http://new.music.yahoo.com/ludacris/news/ludacris-says-he-wanted-lauryn-hill-for-sexes-cd--62000320

"Luda Wears Confederate Flag at Vibe Awards…and Explains Why!" http://slumz.boxden.com/f87/nov-16-luda-wears-confederate-flag-vibe-awards-explains-why-539755/

Mar, Alex. "Ludacris Puts On 'Light.' " *Rolling Stone*, November 12, 2004. http://www.rollingstone.com/music/news/ludacris-puts-on-light-20041112

Reid, Shaheem. "Wall Street Luda Celebrates New Deals: Therapy LP, Radio Show, DTP Comp." *VH1 News*, September 29, 2005. http://www.vh1.com/news/articles/1510639/20050929/index.jhtml

Wolfe, Roman, and Joe Walker. "Exclusive: Ludacris Says New Album 'Ludaversal' Is on Another Level." *All Hip-Hop*, April 25, 2011. http://allhiphop.com/stories/news/archive/2011/04/25/22689692.aspx

On the Internet

Disturbing Tha Peace Records
http://dtprecords.com/

Hip-Hop Summit Action Network
http://www.hsan.org/

Island Def Jam: Ludacris
http://www.islanddefjam.com/artist/home.aspx?artistID=7310

Ludacris Biography
http://www.notablebiographies.com/newsmakers2/2007-Li-Pr/Ludacris.html

The Ludacris Foundation
http://www.theludacrisfoundation.org/

Ludacris World
http://www.ludacrisworld.com

MTV: Ludacris
http://www.mtv.com/music/artist/ludacris/artist.jhtml

INDEX